All about MUSIC

THE ANSWERS TO THE QUESTIONS
YOU HAVEN'T THOUGHT ABOUT

Copyright © 2024 by WhyWhatHuh

All rights reserved.

No part of this book may be reproduced, distributed, or transmitted in any form or by any means, including photocopying, recording, or other electronic or mechanical methods, without the prior written permission of the publisher, except in the case of brief quotations embodied in critical reviews and certain other non-commercial uses permitted by copyright law. For permission requests, write to the publisher, addressed "Attention: Permissions Coordinator," at the address below.

2 Edition

Legal Notice:

While the author has made every effort to ensure the accuracy of the information contained in this book, the information is provided without warranty, express or implied. Neither the author nor the publisher shall be held liable for any damages caused directly or indirectly by the information contained in this book.

Music is the language of the spirit. It opens the secret of life bringing peace, abolishing strife.

Kahlil Gibran

CONTENT

Introduction	6
The WHATs	9
1. What is the "Mozart Effect" and can it really boost baby brains?	10
2. What metal instrument was once crafted from weapons?	12
3. What's the oldest song we know about, and can we still hear it?	14
4. What instrument can you play without touching it?	16
5. What do whale songs and chart-toppers share?	18
6. What skill could link you to Beethoven?	20
7. What cat-inspired music genre hit the scene in the 1600s?	22
8. What music notes look more like artwork?	24
9. What's behind music making us tear up?	26
10. What secret language did the Beatles invent for a song?	28
11. What country is the surprising polka champion?	30
12. What culture first created a musical scale?	32
Myth Smashers	34
The WHYs	37
1. Why do "earworms" get songs stuck in our heads?	38
2. Why is the "Devil's Interval" frowned upon in music?	40
3. Why do we naturally tap our feet to certain rhythms?	42
4. Why does music therapy heal so effectively?	44
5. Why did NASA send music into space on a golden record?	46
6. Why do sad songs make us oddly happy?	48
7. Why do lullabies calm babies everywhere?	50
8. Why does classical music make some squirm?	52

9. Why are so many love songs about breakups? 54
10. Why do bagpipes often play at funerals? 56
11. Why use music in rain-making rituals? 58
12. Why do some animals dance to music? 60
    Myth Smashers 62

The HOWs 65

1. How does a DJ blend songs seamlessly? 66
2. How did a pigeon get an opera singer signed? 68
3. How do blind musicians read music? 70
4. How does our brain treat music differently from speech? 72
5. How did a folk tune become a national anthem? 74
6. How do emotions in music cross cultures? 76
7. How did one note cause the longest lawsuit in music? 78
8. How does a movie score play with your emotions? 80
9. How did music piracy change the industry forever? 82
10. How is silence a composer's secret weapon? 84
11. How did music help bring down the Berlin Wall? 86
12. How does music boost athletic performance? 88
    Myth Smashers 90

The WHENs 93

1. When was the first music festival a hit? 94
2. When did the electric guitar electrify rock 'n' roll? 96
3. When did humans first dance to music? 98
4. When did the saxophone jazz things up? 100
5. When did karaoke become a global craze? 102
6. When did MTV air its first music video? 104

7. When did we first hear the spooky theremin? 106

8. When did streaming overtake album sales? 108

9. When did rap break into the mainstream? 110

10. When was the first opera written and by whom? 112

11. When did vinyl records make a comeback? 114

12. When did live music become big business? 116
Myth Smashers 118

The HUHs 121

1. Huh?! Ever heard of a silent disco with headphone dancers? 122

2. Huh?! Why do some frogs drum like percussionists? 124

3. Huh?! Can plants really groove to tunes and grow better? 126

4. Huh?! There's a record for a concert lasting 453 hours? 128

5. Huh?! Why did a symphony have people break stuff? 130

6. Huh?! Can music change how food tastes? 132

7. Huh?! Why does a song play nonstop in a Hawaiian lava tube? 134

8. Huh?! Did you know there are beetles named after famous musicians? 136

9. Huh?! Can a song be dangerous at certain frequencies? 138

10. Huh?! Why do little birds mimic musical instruments? 140

11. Huh?! A city once got fined for being too quiet? 142

12. Huh?! Can music be used as money, and has it ever? 144
Myth Smashers 146

5 | WHY WHAT HUH?!

Introduction

Welcome to "All About Music," a journey through the wild, quirky, and downright surprising world of music. For most of us, music is a friendly face—whether it's a catchy song on the radio or a concert on a warm summer night. But beyond the tunes and words we know lies a universe full of stories that will make you sit up, laugh, or maybe even hum in awe.

Ever think your favorite jam might change how your dinner tastes? Or that a pigeon could help make an opera singer famous? In this book, we tackle these questions and more, uncovering the magic of music—a language without borders or limits. Some beats make your feet move on their own. And yes, there truly was a concert that lasted 453 hours straight!

We wander through the tales of instruments that started as weapons and the hidden messages in

Beatle songs. You'll learn why NASA thought music was a must-have for space, packing a golden record for a cosmic trip. Get ready to plunge into a world of surprises, where every page brings a new note. So, hit play, and let's dive into this grand medley of wonders!

The WHATs

Where words fail, music speaks.

- Kahlil Gibran

1. What is the "Mozart Effect" and can it really boost baby brains?

The "Mozart Effect" is the idea that listening to the tunes of Mozart can make you smarter. Imagine this: you hit play on some Mozart, and suddenly your baby starts calculating square roots—an instant genius, all thanks to a little symphony. Sounds great, right?

This story kicked off in the 1990s. Some researchers found that college students did better on certain tests after listening to Mozart. The media turned this into a big deal, suggesting Mozart was some magic juice for growing brains.

But can Mozart actually supercharge your child's brain? The scientific answer is: not really. Later studies showed any boost from listening to Mozart is likely small and short-lived. And it's not just Mozart—any music that lifts your mood might give a tiny, temporary brain boost.

The truth is, while music can make life richer and help with some learning, it isn't a magic key to high IQs. Real brain growth happens with a mix of things—reading, playing, exploring, and, yes, enjoying music too.

So, playing Mozart might not create a child prodigy, but it's a lovely way to add some music to your baby's world. Who knows, today's tunes might inspire tomorrow's musician. At the very least, it's a nice song for both of you to enjoy. Genius not required!

2. What metal instrument was once crafted from weapons?

Imagine walking into a room and being handed a musical instrument made from an old weapon. You might think twice before playing it, right? But here's the kicker: this remarkable transformation happened with the trombone in the 19th century. Fascinating, isn't it?

The trombone, with its sliding parts and deep, rich sounds, was once made from recycled weapons. During wars, brass was in high demand. Cannons and swords, once used to fight battles, were melted down and turned into instruments. This was like recycling at its most musical. Quite the makeover!

After conflicts ended, there was often a pile of leftover brass from artillery shells and other weapons. Clever musicians and instrument makers saw a chance. Imagine those metal pieces going from causing chaos to creating symphonies. It's a new life for old war tools.

The trombone is a wonder of physics. Its slide lets musicians hit lots of notes, making it super flexible. When made from old weapons, it symbolized something beautiful: turning war tools into music tools. And that's a transformation worth hearing about.

It wasn't just the trombone that went through this change up. But it does have one of the richest histories. Next time you hear that brassy sound in a jazz band or orchestra, think of the trombone's past life. It shows how people can create beauty even from the roughest beginnings.

So, while that trombone might not fire cannonballs anymore, it sure can send out some powerful notes. And isn't that a much better kind of blast?

3. What's the oldest song we know about, and can we still hear it?

The oldest song we know about isn't topping any music charts today, but it definitely has a special place in history. Meet the "Hurrian Hymn No. 6"—a 3,400-year-old tune from ancient Ugarit, now part of modern-day Syria. Picture it as the hit single of the 14th century BCE.

This ancient song was chiseled into clay tablets using cuneiform—imagine it as an early version of sheet music, albeit in a language that requires an Indiana Jones-level decoder. Discovered by archaeologists in the 1950s, these tablets have been silently humming away for millennia.

So, can we still hear this old melody today? Well, sort of. The ancient notes and language are so cryptic that scholars have had to spend years deciphering them. The hymn honors Nikkal, the goddess of orchards, asking for bountiful harvests—a request that wouldn't seem out of place at today's farmer's market.

Different musicians and researchers have tried to bring the song back to life. Each version sounds a bit different, depending on how they read the ancient script and the musical scale. So, while it won't be your next pop favorite, we can still catch its haunting beauty through these modern attempts.

Listening to the Hurrian Hymn feels like eavesdropping on music time traveled through the ages just to reach us. It's a reminder that while musical trends change, the urge to express through song is truly timeless. Next time you're mixing up your music playlist, remember this old tune paved the way for all the melodies you love today.

4. What instrument can you play without touching it?

The instrument you can play without ever laying a finger on it is the theremin. This isn't a wizard's gadget or a sci-fi movie prop—it's a real musical instrument. Invented in the 1920s by a Russian physicist named Leon Theremin, the theremin is famous for its spooky, ghost-like sounds. Think of the eerie background music in old horror films. Yep, that's probably a theremin.

Imagine an old radio with two antennas: a straight one on the right and a looped one on the left. To play it, you simply wave your hands in the air near these antennas. No touching required! Your right hand controls the pitch. Move closer for high notes and farther for low ones. The left hand? It's all about volume—how loud or soft you want the sound.

So, how does this magic happen? It's all about electromagnetic fields. The antennas create these fields, and your hands change them when moving around. This interaction changes the musical notes, making you a kind of conductor of invisible forces instead of a regular musician.

The theremin isn't just for spooky tunes. Serious musicians love it too. It's tricky to master, needing a keen ear and steady hands. But, once you get it, it's incredibly rewarding.

From those creepy movie soundscapes to cutting-edge performances, the theremin shows us that sometimes, making music is as simple as a wave of the hand. Who knew you could make music by just waving your hands in the air? It's almost like having a bit of wizardry up your sleeve.

5. What do whale songs and chart-toppers share?

Whale songs and chart-toppers might seem like they come from different worlds, but they share some surprising tunes. Dive into this musical mystery, and you'll discover some intriguing similarities.

Picture this: a whale, the ocean's superstar, singing a tune that echoes through the deep. Just like pop stars who aim for the next big hit, male humpback whales sing to attract a mate. Their songs are like complex musicals, changing over time with new beats and grooves—a sea version of "Greatest Hits," if you will. Think of it as going viral, but with sound waves drifting through salty water.

Both whale songs and chart-toppers love repetition. It's the trick that lodges tunes in your brain, whether you're a fish with fins or a person with a playlist. For whales, repeating melodies helps spread their "message"—to attract mates or warn rivals. For humans, repetitive hooks in pop songs make them easy to sing in the shower or get stuck in your head while you scroll through memes.

There's more. Both whale songs and pop music ride the wave of cultural shifts. Whales from different parts of the ocean have unique songs. These songs can change over time, much like musical trends jumping from disco to hip-hop. Songs take on new elements, like a remix, blending the old with the fresh.

In the end, whether it's a whale crooning below the waves or a pop star dazzling the crowd, both aim for that magic moment. The moment when their audience—whether it's another whale or a crowd of fans—stops and listens intently. Next time you're hooked by a catchy tune on the radio, think of the humpback whales, the original ocean rockstars, who've been singing chart-toppers long before we ever picked up a guitar. Who needs a Grammy when your stage is the entire ocean?

6. What skill could link you to Beethoven?

Imagine for a moment, stepping into the shoes of Beethoven himself. You're at the piano, deep in thought, ready to create music that will last for centuries. But how do you connect with a musical legend who couldn't hear his own music in the end? Through the fascinating skill of "musical visualization."

Musical visualization is like playing a piano in your mind, imagining your living room as Vienna's grandest concert hall. It's hearing music in your head without actually hearing it aloud. Beethoven was a master at this, composing whole symphonies in his imagination despite being deaf. Like writing a story without putting down a single word—just keeping it alive in your mind.

Think of musical visualization as mental exercises for your ears. It gets your brain's sound-processing part working hard, bringing melodies to life purely from imagination. You might think this skill is just for music pros, but science shows it's not. Many musicians practice this way, improving their skills without even touching their instruments. Silent, but effective.

And here's the twist. Anyone can get the hang of it. You don't need to be a Beethoven. Start by imagining your favorite song and play it in your mind. It might not be the next "Ode to Joy," but with practice, you can impress friends with your silent music skills at the next gathering.

So, if you find yourself imagining music during a boring moment, you've got a little Beethoven in you. Let your mind be your orchestra and your imagination the conductor. Your mental sonatas could just be music to your ears—or at least to your brain!

7. What cat-inspired music genre hit the scene in the 1600s?

Back in the 1600s, Europe's music scene saw something unusual: a playful genre inspired by our furry feline friends. Known as "cat music," it was a mix of sounds that could make any cat's whiskers twitch with joy.

In Italy, this cat-themed craze took off largely because of composer Domenico Scarlatti. Scarlatti wasn't just fond of cats; he let one become his co-composer. His cat, Pulcinella, would prance across the harpsichord, hitting random notes. Instead of shooing her away, Scarlatti listened. He turned her accidental melodies into the lively "Fuga del Gatto" or "Cat's Fugue." The piece captures the unpredictable antics of a cat dancing on a keyboard.

The charm of cat music went beyond its playful notes. At a time when music was all about rules and order, this genre brought in fun and surprise. It showed that music could be as unpredictable as a cat hiding in a basket.

Today, "cat music" might not top the charts, but its place in history is a funny reminder of how creativity can spring from the most unexpected muses. Next time you hear a piano piece with a playful touch, think of Pulcinella, the original keyboard kitty. Inspiration can really come from anywhere—even from a cat that naps all day!

8. What music notes look more like artwork?

Music notes are more than just sounds ready to be heard; they're tiny pieces of art with their own style. Treble clefs are the stars of this show. With their swirling lines and fancy loops, they could easily belong on an abstract artist's canvas.

Key signatures, on the other hand, are like mysterious codes. Made up of sharps and flats, they spread beautifully across the page like an ancient script. They have this secretive charm, inviting us to wonder about the hidden tunes they hold.

Then we have time signatures. Simple fractions on the page, they control the beat and pace of a piece with almost clock-like accuracy. Like the Swiss watches of music notation—small, yet incredibly precise.

Let's not overlook the everyday notes, especially the whole note. Its fancy relative, the dotted half note, adds a bit of style, like a beauty mark on a glamorous movie star. These notes balance form and function, much like a well-designed piece of furniture.

And there are ties and slurs, those gentle curves that connect notes in a graceful flow. They act as smooth bridges in the world of music, adding elegance and a sense of fluidity, like a beautiful dance.

Together, these elements create a visual symphony as well as an auditory one. Each note and symbol is a small piece of art, showing off human creativity. Music might be the universal language of mankind, but its notes are universal doodles, proving art exists even in the notes of a song. Next time you look at a sheet of music, take a moment to enjoy the view. Your ears—and your eyes—will be glad you did.

9. What's behind music making us tear up?

When music makes tears sneak out of our eyes, it's not just because Adele nails those high notes. The reason music makes us cry is a curious mix of science, feelings, and hormones, all dancing around in our brains.

First, let's look at the brain's hotspot for emotions: the limbic system. This area lights up when we listen to music, especially those heart-touching tunes. It's like your brain is having its own emotional party—cue the violins! When the limbic system gets excited, it tells the nervous system to join in, causing goosebumps and watery eyes.

Then there's dopamine, the "feel-good" chemical in our brains. When a song hits just right, dopamine floods our system. This rush feels like the joy of eating chocolate or cracking a tough puzzle.

Plus, memories step in. Songs can whisk us back to important moments, stirring up old emotions. That's why the first notes of a song can feel like meeting a long-lost friend—or rival.

Cultural habits also play a role. Certain musical patterns make us cry. Minor chords and descending melodies often sound sad because we've learned to link them with sorrow.

Musicians, with some tricks up their sleeves, use things like "appoggiatura"—a fancy word for making tension in music. This creates a little musical sigh, pulling emotions from even the toughest hearts.

In the end, the dance between music and tears is a beautiful mix of biology and memories. So next time a song brings out the tissues, remember, it's not just the music. It's your brain celebrating a festival of feelings. And there's nothing wrong with enjoying a little emotional encore.

10. What secret language did the Beatles invent for a song?

The Beatles were more than just musical geniuses; they were quite the playful bunch too. Among their many quirks, they dreamed up their own kind of secret language. For the song "Sun King" on the Abbey Road album, they mixed English, Italian, Spanish, and a whole lot of imaginative gobbledygook.

John Lennon, the mastermind behind this unique creation, wanted something that sounded like foreign languages but didn't make sense in any one tongue. Think of it like your cat meowing a sonnet—fun and imaginative, but not exactly something you'd submit for a language exam.

Take the phrase "Cuando para mucho mi amore de felice corazón." It doesn't mean anything sensible in Spanish, Italian, or any other language. Instead, it strings together words that sound dreamy and exotic. It's a bit like dipping into a surrealist's dream book.

So, why did they do it? Maybe they just wanted to have a laugh, a cheeky wink to the cultures and languages they loved. Or maybe they were embracing the wild spirit of the 60s, full of experiments and psychedelic vibes.

This playful mix adds mystery to "Sun King," letting fans wonder about its meaning—or if it even has one. It's a reminder that sometimes, the fun is simply in listening and not decoding.

In the end, the Beatles' word adventure in "Sun King" is like a good joke. It might not make complete sense, but it's utterly delightful. Next time someone insists on things making sense, channel your inner Beatle. Remember, a bit of joyful nonsense can speak volumes, even in a made-up language.

11. What country is the surprising polka champion?

In the dance world, where elegance and rhythm play together, you might expect the polka—a lively and cheerful dance often linked to countries like Poland—to have obvious champions. But when it comes to global polka stars, the winner might just be, surprisingly, the Philippines.

Yes, the Philippines—a nation better known for its love of karaoke—has become a standout in the polka scene. You might wonder how this island group, far from Europe, took to this bouncy dance. The answer is as fun as a polka dot, thanks to centuries of cultural mixing.

Back in the 16th century, when Spain began its long stay in the Philippines, it brought along European dances. Polka was among them. The Filipinos, always quick to embrace new things, mixed it with their own traditions. Over time, they created their own version of polka, now a staple at festivals and parties throughout the islands.

What makes Filipino polka so special? It's the blend of old and new. While keeping the fast steps and happy beats, it adds native outfits and sometimes local tunes. This makes it a unique cultural mix that's truly Filipino. The dance is alive and well, from Luzon to Mindanao, showcasing the joyful spirit of its people.

In a world full of cultural exchanges, the Philippines' love for polka is a toe-tapping surprise. Next time you're tapping your foot to a polka tune, think of the sunny Philippine islands. Here, polka isn't just a dance—it's a tale of cultural fusion. Who knew polka could be such a sweet surprise? Where there's a will to dance, there's a way to win, even on the other side of the globe!

12. What culture first created a musical scale?

Tracing the origins of the musical scale is like trying to find the original recipe for pizza—everyone wants a slice of the credit, and the truth is deliciously messy. The creation of musical scales likely wasn't a solo act. Instead, it was a global jam session, with different cultures adding their own unique ingredients.

Let's start in ancient Mesopotamia. Over 4,000 years ago, the Sumerians were busy carving musical notes onto clay tablets. They used scales similar to our modern do-re-mi system. This heptatonic, or seven-note, scale was a stepping stone to future musical adventures.

Zoom over to the ancient Greeks. Pythagoras in the 6th century BCE wasn't just working on triangles. He was also figuring out the sounds between notes. His work in harmonics was key in shaping modern scales.

Onward to India, where music had its own flavors. The Indian scales, or ragas, were detailed and expressive. Each raga aimed to create a different mood. They weren't just tunes; they were spiritual journeys.

And don't overlook China. Even Confucius thought music brought social harmony. The Chinese came up with a five-note scale. It's a simple pattern with timeless appeal.

Every culture had its own beat and reasons for making scales. They might have been counting stars or jotting down poetry, but people have always looked for ways to shape sound that fits their world.

In the end, musical scales are like nature's kaleidoscope. Beautiful patterns from a simple twist. Whoever first crafted a scale, their notes echo through time. They've turned into a universal language that still gets everyone tapping their feet today.

Myth Smashers

✗ **MYTH:**

Classical music is only for the elite and highly educated.

✓ **FACT:**

Classical music is for everyone. It doesn't matter who you are or where you're from. Many people enjoy the deep sounds and feelings it brings. It's like looking at a beautiful painting; you don't need to be an art expert to love it.

✗ **MYTH:**

You need natural talent to learn music.

✓ **FACT:**

Learning music is about building skills, not just showing off talent. Just like riding a bike, it takes practice and patience. Anyone can learn music, just like anyone can learn to ride.

The WHYs

Music can change the world because it can change people.

— Hans Christian Andersen

1. Why do "earworms" get songs stuck in our heads?

Earworms. They might sound like annoying little bugs, but they're really just those tunes that lodge themselves in your brain, playing over and over. These catchy songs are the ones you hum in the shower, at work, or when trying to mime something tricky. So, why do they stick around like a song on repeat?

To crack this mystery, let's peek into the world of brain science. An earworm is what's known as "involuntary musical imagery." Basically, it's a catchy tune that takes over your brain's music center and refuses to leave. These song invaders often have simple tunes, repetitive beats, and unexpected turns, just like that pop song you can't help but sing along to.

One idea is that earworms cling to us because our brains love patterns and repetition. It's as if our minds become detectives, replaying the melody to solve some sort of unsolved musical case. They tend to sneak in during boring tasks, like brushing your teeth or waiting for the bus. In these moments, our brains—kinda like a playground—let these musical visitors swing from one brain cell to the next.

But there's more. Studies suggest that earworms can be stirred by feelings or connections. Maybe a song played during a memorable school dance or at a favorite café on holiday. These songs get stored in your brain, wrapped with a bow of emotion. When you're in a similar situation or mood, your brain hits play, thinking it's being helpful.

How do you break free from this musical loop? Some say finishing the song in your head or doing tricky tasks, like solving a puzzle, can help shift your brain's focus. But do we really want to ditch them so fast? A world with no surprise mini-concerts in your head might be a tad too quiet.

So, next time you catch a tune stuck in your mind, just go with it. It's your brain's quirky way of making music. And honestly, who doesn't get a kick out of being the star of their own little concert?

2. Why is the "Devil's Interval" frowned upon in music?

The "Devil's Interval," or tritone, has been a bit of a troublemaker in music for ages. This spooky sound stretches over three whole tones, creating a gap that's too wide for comfort—like trying to fit on a too-small hammock. Back in medieval times, when music was all about calm and peace, anything that sounded like a musical cry for help was a no-go.

Why the bad rap? The tritone sits awkwardly between notes that usually sound nice together, creating a clash. It's like biting into a lemon when you were expecting an orange—surprising and a bit sour. This made early composers nervous, branding it "diabolus in musica," or the devil in music. They stayed clear of it, much like avoiding a piano with a few broken keys.

But not everyone saw it that way. Many non-Western music traditions welcomed the tritone. It didn't scare them at all. In fact, they saw it as charming, like a lovable rogue. Even Western music eventually changed its tune. In the 20th century, composers started to love the tritone for its dramatic flair—just ask any jazz musician or heavy metal guitarist.

Today, the tritone is more of a cheeky character than a villain. It adds intrigue, just like a twist in a detective story. So, while it was once seen as devilish, it's now a fascinating musical adventurer. Next time you hear it, think of it not as evil but as exciting—a sound that went from outcast to trailblazer, leading music on wild adventures.

3. Why do we naturally tap our feet to certain rhythms?

Have you ever caught yourself tapping your feet or nodding your head to a catchy tune? You're definitely not alone. Humans have a special connection to music; it's like an invisible string pulling us to the beat. But what's behind this urge to keep rhythm with our bodies?

Our brains are big fans of patterns. Music is one of the most delightful patterns we know. When we hear a steady rhythm, our brains start to make predictions, like a fortune teller who's always right. Each time a beat hits just when expected, we get a little burst of dopamine, that feel-good brain juice that makes us smile inside.

This rhythm magic is all about biology. The motor cortex, a part of our brain usually busy with movement, lights up even when we're just listening to music. It seems our brains are sneakily getting us ready for a dance party—even if we're just sitting still. This link between hearing and moving explains why even babies, who can't walk yet, will wiggle to a beat. It's nature's way of prepping us to boogie.

And it's not just us humans. Some animals, like parrots and elephants, feel the rhythm too. Although, they probably won't be joining a dance contest anytime soon. Still, being able to groove to a beat isn't just a human thing.

So, why does rhythm matter so much? In ancient times, syncing up with others helped our ancestors work together, like paddling a canoe or hunting as a team. Imagine trying to do those things without timing—it'd be a mess!

Next time your foot starts tapping along to a tune, recall this: it's more than just fun. You're part of a complex dance involving your brain, evolution, and good vibes. It's a lively mix of neurons and notes, showing us that life, like music, is all about getting the rhythm right. So whether you're a toe-tapper or a full-on dancer, remember it's your brain's way of celebrating the beat. And that, surely, is something to tap about!

4. Why does music therapy heal so effectively?

Music therapy works wonders for the soul, turning tunes into a soothing balm. Think of it like the magic of hearing your favorite song just when you need it most, backed by science. Our brains love music; it's more than just toe-tapping. Music lights up parts of the brain tied to feelings, memories, and even movement.

When you're singing along, your brain rewards you with dopamine, the happy juice. It's the same stuff you feel when you eat your favorite chocolate or hit the jackpot. But music's magic doesn't stop there. It can lower cortisol levels, the stress hormone that lurks around like a bad smell. Less stress, more smiles. Music therapy is like having a wellness coach in your ear.

This therapy is more than just blasting your top hits. It's a personalized mix where therapists use tunes and beats to meet your needs. For example, rhythmic beats can help people with movement disorders get their groove back. Kind of like how you can't resist tapping your foot to a catchy song.

Music also has a knack for unlocking memories, especially for those with conditions like Alzheimer's.

Old songs can bring back memories that words cannot, helping people reconnect with their past.

Let's not forget the power of music in groups. Sing-alongs or drumming circles can create a sense of connection. It's a great way to fight off feelings of loneliness and make friends.

In a world where stress pops up like ads online, music therapy offers a simple fix. Next time you're feeling down, maybe try your headphones before reaching for the medicine cabinet. Who knew healing could be as easy as hitting play?

5. Why did NASA send music into space on a golden record?

Imagine you're throwing the ultimate space party. You want to make a killer first impression, right? NASA thought so too when they launched a golden record into the cosmos in 1977. It wasn't just about sending Earth's greatest hits into the void, though. These records were a friendly "Hello!" from us Earthlings to anyone—or anything—out there.

The Voyager probes initially set off to explore the faraway planets. But scientists, with a dash of ambition and a sprinkle of imagination, decided to include a mixtape of Earth's sounds. A truly cosmic compilation. From classics like Bach to Chuck Berry's rockin' "Johnny B. Goode," the record aims to get any alien listener tapping their feet—assuming they have them. There's even a heartwarming "hello" from a mother to her baby and the gentle sound of a kiss. Because who doesn't enjoy a bit of Earthly affection?

But why music and not a plain message? Music is often called a universal language. It shares feelings and culture, even when words fail. In a galaxy far, far away, it says: "Here's a taste of who we are—quirky, emotional, and fond of a great rhythm." Carl Sagan, one of the big thinkers behind this plan, hoped it would show potential alien listeners that humans are full of emotion and creativity—things that might cross any starry boundary.

Now, the truth is, the chance of these records being found is microscopic. The Voyagers are zooming through space at a blazing 38,000 miles per hour. Sounds fast? Well, not when you consider the universe's sheer size. And that's part of the charm. These Golden Records act like messages in a bottle tossed into a vast, cosmic sea. They're a testament to our hopes and dreams.

In the end, whether aliens ever find these records or not, they remind us of something important. They capture a snapshot of humanity's creativity, diversity, and curiosity. If we do get a reply, let's hope those extraterrestrial DJs dig our music—or at least send a request for a remix!

6. Why do sad songs make us oddly happy?

When you catch yourself smiling through tears while jamming to a sad song, it might seem like a strange emotional puzzle. But don't worry, you're not the only one in this tuneful twist. Sad songs have a knack for tugging at our heartstrings while giving us a sneaky happiness boost. And yes, this emotional roller coaster is quite normal.

To dig into this musical mystery, let's look at the science behind sadness. Believe it or not, when you listen to sad songs, your brain gets flooded with a delightful mix of chemicals. Dopamine, the feel-good neurotransmitter, is released. Yep, the same one that lights up your brain when you munch on chocolate or ace a game of Tic-Tac-Toe. So instead of being a downer, sad music can actually lift our spirits.

Sad music also creates a safe space to explore feelings. It's like a heart-to-heart with an old friend with a guitar. We can feel sadness without the real-world mess. It's like watching a sad movie knowing the dog will come back in the end.

Plus, there's a social side. Sharing sad songs makes us feel closer to others. In fact, people often enjoy these tunes more together. It's a way of saying, "I feel you," without any words.

And let's not forget nostalgia. Sad songs remind us of the past—maybe a first heartbreak or those angsty teenage years. This bittersweet memory brings a warm glow, making us feel oddly happy.

So, next time you're tapping your foot with a sniffle to a tearful tune, remember there's a method to this madness. These heart-wrenching harmonies might just be a secret to balancing our emotional diet—like musical broccoli with a touch of ice cream. In the end, it seems sad songs know how to hit the right notes in our hearts, leaving us thankful for the complex beauty of our feelings. And that's music to your ears!

7. Why do lullabies calm babies everywhere?

Lullabies have been parents' secret weapon against restless babies since, well, forever. But why do these tunes work like magic across the globe? Picture being a tiny human, new to the world, with a flood of strange sights and sounds. Then, a lullaby plays—a soothing, repetitive melody that feels like a warm hug, helping little ones feel safe and snug.

There's some science behind this musical magic. Lullabies use rhythm and repetition. Their slow beat mirrors a mother's heartbeat, a familiar sound from womb days. This can slow a baby's heart rate and breathing, leading to calmness. Think of it as the ultimate white noise machine, but with a much sweeter tone.

The tunes of lullabies tend to rise and fall gently, much like how parents speak to their babies. Young ears are especially tuned to these patterns, which can help them drift into sleep. Plus, lullabies are simple—no tricky musical twists to keep a baby's brain too busy to relax.

On the cultural front, while lullabies around the world may sound different, their goal is the same: soothe the baby and, in turn, the parent. Whether it's

"Twinkle Twinkle Little Star" or a French "Berceuse," the heart of the lullaby remains unchanged.

Here's a fun fact: Lullabies aren't just for babies. Singing them can de-stress parents, too. It turns out that singing releases oxytocin, the bonding hormone. So, calming the baby also calms the parent—a win-win.

In the end, lullabies are like magic threads that connect parents and babies in sleepy harmony. It's a simple trick where music meets biology, with a sprinkle of enchantment. And just like that, everyone gets a bit more rest. Sweet dreams!

8. Why does classical music make some squirm?

Classical music can be like an opera singer showing up at your morning coffee shop—unexpected and a bit intense. So, why does it make some of us wriggle in our seats, as if we're on a symphonic rollercoaster? Let's dive in.

The key might be in its complexity. Classical music loves to take the scenic route, weaving long, unpredictable journeys that can feel like a musical puzzle. Pop songs, on the other hand, are like catchy jingles that stick to you like chewing gum. If you're not used to the twists and turns, you might feel a bit like Alice in a symphonic Wonderland.

Our brains add another layer to this puzzle. Music links to our emotions and memories. For some folks, classical tunes might bring back memories of stiff concert seats or childhood piano lessons where each mistake was like setting off a siren. If you picture classical music with the stern gaze of a piano teacher, it's no wonder you might squirm.

Then there's today's culture. Our fast-paced world loves quick hits and instant music fixes. A full symphony? It can feel like stepping into a time machine, back to when patience was more than a virtue—it was essential.

But here's the twist: neuroscientists say classical music can boost brain activity, help you sleep better, and even calm your nerves. So, while it might not be love at first listen, sticking with it could show you its hidden charm.

In the end, maybe squirming is just your body's way of saying it's curious yet confused. Go ahead, embrace the squirm. You might find yourself humming along with Beethoven, not bouncing in discomfort, but tapping in time.

9. Why are so many love songs about breakups?

Love songs and breakups are like peanut butter and jelly—always stuck together. But why do so many love songs zoom in on heartbreak? The answer is all about our hearts and brains.

Let's first look at the emotional ride of a breakup. When a relationship ends, feelings hit the roof. Songwriters, much like expert chefs, mix this blend of emotions to create songs we can't stop singing. Breakups offer a feast of feelings—sadness, longing, anger, and sometimes, relief. These strong feelings make for perfect songs because we humans are wired to connect with deep emotions. Listening to a breakup song is like sharing a tub of ice cream with a friend who truly understands.

And guess what? There's science behind this too. Studies show that when we're heartbroken, our brains react like we've been physically hurt. That's right, a breakup can actually bruise your brain. But this pain makes breakup ballads so captivating. When we're down, just like we crave comfort food, our hearts crave music that gets us. Sad music releases prolactin, a hormone that helps us handle stress. So, breakup songs might actually help us heal. They're like medicine for the soul.

The music business also knows what hits the charts. Songs about love gone wrong have mass appeal—they speak to anyone who's survived a romantic split. Relatable songs sell well because they touch so many people. Breakup songs hit a universal chord, making them a win-win for artists and producers.

And let's not forget the power of a good story. Every gripping story needs conflict, and what better conflict than a breakup? A skillful song about lost love takes us on a journey, letting both songwriters and listeners explore their feelings safely.

So, breakup songs are the heart's way of throwing a perfect pity party. They bring out emotions, soothe our minds, and keep the music industry thriving. Next time you're singing a breakup tune, remember this: you're not just singing about sadness; you're joining in on a healing ritual as old as time. Now, pass the tissues, please.

10. Why do bagpipes often play at funerals?

Picture this: a lone bagpiper, standing on a hillside, playing the sorrowful tune of "Amazing Grace." The sound floats through the air like a gentle sigh. It's a scene almost as iconic as tartan at a Scottish wedding. But why do bagpipes often play at funerals? The answer is a mix of tradition, sound science, and a touch of history, all wrapped up in kilts.

Bagpipes are ancient, popping up in places like Egypt and Rome, but they truly found their home in Scotland. Over time, they've become tied to both celebration and mourning. The sound is unique—some might even say haunting. Bagpipes use an air bag to create a steady, unbroken sound. This drone feels timeless, making it ideal for marking life's passage at funerals.

But there's more than just the sound. History plays a big role, too. During the world wars, Scottish soldiers marched into battle led by bagpipes. When they died, it was fitting that the same powerful music honored their bravery. Bagpipes became a tribute to courage and sacrifice, an audible salute to those who've moved on.

And let's not forget their emotional punch. Bagpipes can stir even the toughest hearts. It might be the high notes pulling on emotions or their ties to Celtic roots and wild landscapes. Whatever the reason, their echoes fill the vast spaces of funeral gatherings, like a musical hug from nature itself.

Interestingly, bagpipes have journeyed beyond Scotland. Irish and American communities have embraced them too. In America, where many have Scottish or Irish roots, they've become part of mournful traditions. Events like police and firefighter funerals often feature pipers, adding honor and solemnity.

So next time you hear bagpipes at a funeral, think of them as a bridge between past and present. They're a nod to bravery and a reminder of life's ongoing circle. Their music strikes a chord, quite literally, showing us that while life may be short, memories last—much like the echo of that final note.

In the end, when it comes to bagpipes at funerals, it's clear they're not just blowing hot air.

11. Why use music in rain-making rituals?

Using music in rain-making rituals may sound like something out of a fantasy story, but it's a mix of old traditions and a sprinkle of science that even doubters might find intriguing. Picture a world where beats and dances have the power to coax the sky into opening up. These rituals, found in cultures around the world, are the ultimate rainmakers' jam sessions—where community spirit meets the big wish for rain.

First, let's look at the cultural side. Music and dance have always been central to how humans express themselves—way before the days of Spotify playlists. In rain-making rituals, music is the universal language. It matches human hopes with nature's own rhythms. The drumming, singing, and melodies aren't just random sounds. They unite people, strengthen community bonds, and send a collective message to the skies that it's time for a little drizzle or downpour.

From a science angle, there's no clear-cut link between your favorite rain dance song and real rain. But, these rituals do have an indirect effect. They boost community spirit and optimism, making people more resilient. Some might even wonder if the vibrations from music could change atmospheric conditions. But let's be honest, we wouldn't suggest relying on your Bluetooth speaker to fix a drought just yet.

Interestingly, the relationship between water and sound isn't total nonsense. Sound waves travel through water, and certain vibrations can make real changes. Scientists even see this in experiments where sound affects how liquids behave. While the idea of music making rain might be a bit magical, it's a fun thought.

So, while your local weather expert probably won't trade in their radar for a rain dance playlist, there's more to these rituals than you might think. Next time you get caught in a sudden rain shower, pause for a moment. Maybe, just maybe, somewhere a group is striking up their ritual music, putting on the best rain request concert we'll never attend.

12. Why do some animals dance to music?

When it comes to animals getting their groove on, it's not just about a catchy beat. The sight of a cockatoo bopping along to the Backstreet Boys or a sea lion shimmying to Shakira makes us wonder: why do some animals dance to music?

First, let's dive into the science. The ability to move in time with a rhythm, known as "entrainment," has a lot to do with brains that can learn and copy sounds. This means some creatures, like birds and maybe even some mammals, are wired to react to tunes because their brains link sounds with movement. Parrots, known for copying human voices, are at the top of the animal dance charts thanks to these skills. But they aren't alone. Sea lions have also shown they can keep a beat, despite not being the best at imitating sounds.

Why is this? Just like us, these animals might find certain music rewarding or exciting. Dancing might be less about showing off their rhythm and more about the sheer fun of it. In simpler terms, they're enjoying themselves, not trying out for an animal talent show.

Interestingly, research suggests that animals who can match a beat don't do it for survival or evolution—

unlike a lion's roar or a peacock's tail. Instead, it's a wonderful side effect of having a complex brain, almost like a bonus feature.

In the end, dancing animals show us that nature loves a good jam session too. Next time you see a parrot tapping its claw or a sea lion bobbing along, remember that rhythm crosses species lines. It seems animals have more in common with us than we think—especially in cutting loose and having fun. So, who leads the animal dance party next? Maybe the elephants—they may be big, but word has it they have some smooth moves up their trunks.

Myth Smashers

✘ **MYTH:**

Good music needs to be complex with hidden meanings.

✓ **FACT:**

Simple music often touches hearts more deeply. Many popular songs are straightforward yet powerful, like a simple but gripping tale.

✘ **MYTH:**

Listening to classical music makes babies smarter (Mozart Effect).

✓ **FACT:**

While it's a nice idea, there's no proof that Mozart or other classical music boosts brainpower. It can calm and delight, like a lullaby, but it won't magically make you a genius.

The HOWs

How is it that music can, without words, evoke our laughter, our fears, our highest aspirations?

- Bono

1. How does a DJ blend songs seamlessly?

DJs have a special talent for making music blend together, like a smooth river of sound at a dance party. But how do they pull this off? No secret potions needed here! It's all about rhythm, timing, and a bit of tech, with a sprinkle of musical smarts.

The DJ's magic wand is the mixer. Think of it as the conductor's baton, deciding which tune takes center stage and which one slides into the shadows. To blend songs, DJs use two main tricks: beatmatching and crossfading.

Beatmatching is the art of getting two songs to march to the same beat. Sounds simple? Not quite, especially with different beats and tempos. DJs tweak the tempo on their turntables or software, syncing the pulse of two tracks to beat as one. It's like getting two hearts to sync up in perfect rhythm—rather romantic, don't you think?

Crossfading is the smooth master of transition, making the switch from one song to the next seamless. With a gentle glide of the fader, a DJ lowers the volume of the outgoing track while raising the one coming in. It's like a musical handoff so smooth you barely notice the change, much like passing a baton seamlessly in a relay race.

Now, technology steps in to help. Modern DJ software offers an assist, syncing beats automatically and suggesting songs that match in tempo and key. It's like having a digital co-pilot whispering tips in your ear. But it's the DJ's own flair and taste that make the mix pop. They pick tracks that don't just match in tempo but also vibe well together, creating an exciting musical journey.

A DJ's work mixes art with a dash of science. They're part human metronome, part musical chef, crafting a tasty sound mix that keeps us moving. Next time you're lost in a perfect mix, remember: there's more than luck spinning those decks. It's a rhythm-fueled dance of beats, bars, and beats-per-minute. Keep dancing!

2. How did a pigeon get an opera singer signed?

In the world of opera, pigeons aren't exactly what you'd expect to make headlines. But, believe it or not, one plucky pigeon helped an opera singer hit the big time. Curious how that came about?

Picture this: Fat Lady Sings, a vibrant opera production in bustling New York City. Among the eager performers was an aspiring singer with a voice as smooth as silk, but still waiting for her big chance. Enter the pigeon—just an ordinary bird, or so it seemed. This pigeon had made a cozy nest up in the rafters where auditions were being held.

Pigeons, believe it or not, have a fascinating history as nature's original messengers. Long before emails, pigeons carried important messages. But our pigeon wasn't delivering letters; it was bringing sheer luck. During a tense audition, our singer nailed a note so powerful that it startled the pigeon from its perch. Whoosh! It swooped through the auditorium like a mini drama all its own.

This unexpected spectacle grabbed the attention of every judge in the room. Capturing attention is half the battle in showbiz, and our singer did it with flair, thanks to her feathery co-star. Soon after, she found herself signing a coveted opera contract. (The pigeon, for its part, went back to its rooftop perch.)

This tale is a delightful reminder of how unpredictable life can be. Success often needs more than just talent or hard work. Sometimes, it takes a dash of luck—even if it flutters in on pigeon wings. So, next time you're in a tough spot, remember: help might come from the most unexpected places. Listen for cooing in the rafters; it just might signal something extraordinary.

3. How do blind musicians read music?

Blind musicians have a unique way of "reading" music, and it's a bit like magic. It's called Braille music, a clever system where raised dots translate into the notes and rhythms of everything from Beethoven to jazz. Louis Braille, the genius behind this system, was a blind Frenchman who didn't let a lack of sight stop him from revolutionizing how blind people read. He extended his invention, Braille, into the realm of music, giving notes their own special "dot-code."

Using Braille music is all about touch. Imagine feeling dots on a page that tell you the exact note to play. Musicians slide their fingers over these dots, figuring out each note one at a time. It's like solving a puzzle piece by piece, but with music.

Learning Braille music isn't easy; it's like picking up a new language. Yet, once you learn it, it unlocks the entire orchestra just for you. Many blind musicians memorize the music as they go, weaving the pattern of notes into their memory.

And then there's technology, always ready to add a twist. New software can turn sheet music into audio or display it in Braille, putting a whole library of music at their fingertips. This opens up endless musical possibilities.

So, when you see a musician gliding their fingers over those dots, know they're creating a symphony in their mind, note by note. Braille music transforms invisible notes into something you can hear. It's a wonderful reminder of how curiosity finds its way, turning seemingly impossible challenges into beautiful melodies.

4. How does our brain treat music differently from speech?

The brain works like a savvy DJ, tuning into the rhythm of life with a playlist that includes both music and speech. While music and speech might seem similar, like two sides of the same coin, your brain treats them quite differently.

When you hear music, it's like your brain's right side has been invited to a party. This part loves the tunes and beats—it's your brain's personal dance floor, diving into the sound with excitement. Music taps into our feelings, lighting up the brain's reward centers. This might explain why a catchy tune can feel as good as a sunny day.

Speech, on the other hand, is processed on the brain's left side, where the serious work happens. This part decodes words and sentences like a skilled editor, cutting through the noise to get the message. Ever notice how you can follow a chat but struggle with song lyrics? That's your brain focusing on speech, deciding when to nod or smile.

Interestingly, music and speech do have some common ground. The brain uses rhythm for both. This might be why some people memorize song lyrics faster than their grocery list. Patterns, it seems, are like a universal language for our minds.

In short, your brain is both a musician and a writer, juggling all the sounds it hears every day. It's a bit like having a split personality, in the friendliest way. So, next time a pop song gets stuck in your head, thank your brain for needing a musical break from the everyday noise. Who knew it had such a taste for variety?

5. How did a folk tune become a national anthem?

Turning a folk tune into a national anthem is a bit like asking your friendly neighbor to run for class president—unexpected, but sometimes it just works wonders. Take "La Marseillaise," the national anthem of France. Before it became the anthem we link with revolutions, it was more like the hit song of its time.

Back in 1792, when France was knee-deep in the French Revolutionary Wars, a military officer named Claude Joseph Rouget de Lisle composed a lively tune. It wasn't meant to be a grand anthem at first. Just a rallying cry for soldiers, full of images of bursting tyrants and thirsty fields—metaphorically speaking. It struck a chord with the people's spirit and spread like wildfire.

People loved it. Not just for its dramatic words about liberty and unity, but because it had a tune everyone could hum. Like the "Baby Shark" of 18th-century France. As the revolution rolled on, "La Marseillaise" became the music of the movement. Crowds sang it with passion, waving their flags in the air.

Without social media to make things go viral, word of mouth carried the song from town to town. Soon, it caught the attention of those in charge. By 1795, "La Marseillaise" was officially named the national anthem of France. It journeyed from a local hit to a symbol of national pride.

This tale isn't just France's. The U.S. had "The Star-Spangled Banner," once an old English drinking song, chosen as its anthem in 1931. Music, simple yet strong, can unite a country, a fascinating fact.

So next time you're humming a catchy folk tune, remember: it's not just a song. It might be a future anthem waiting for its big moment. History reminds us: from folk to official takes just a few sing-alongs!

6. How do emotions in music cross cultures?

Imagine walking into a music festival where bands come from all over the world. You might hear the soft sound of a sitar or the lively beats of a djembe. Even if you don't understand the words, you can probably tell if a song is happy, sad, or something else. This ability to "feel" music's emotion, even without understanding the lyrics, is quite fascinating. How do emotions in music reach across cultures?

Music is like a universal language that everyone can understand—kind of like a global game of charades, but with way cooler soundtracks. Researchers have found that certain music features bring out similar feelings in people everywhere. Fast music in a major key usually means happiness. Slow music in a minor key often means sadness. It's like our ears come with an emotional guidebook for music.

Why does this happen? It's a mix of biology and culture. Our brains are wired to react to sounds that have always signaled emotions, like a soothing voice or a scary growl. But culture also shapes how we feel about music. It teaches us to connect certain sounds with emotions, like the spooky music in horror movies that makes us grip our seats.

Music also copies the way we speak. High notes can mean excitement or fear. Low notes might mean calmness or danger. This is why, whether you're in Kathmandu or Kansas, a rising melody can give you butterflies or chills.

Of course, not every tune fits perfectly into these categories. Some styles, like the strange sounds of avant-garde jazz, don't follow the usual rules. It's like trying to solve a puzzle blindfolded. Yet, listeners can often figure out the feelings through instruments and volume changes.

In the end, music's ability to share feelings across cultures shows how it connects us all. Despite our differences, we all move to a similar beat. So next time you're at that worldwide festival, let your heart guide you. Whether it's samba, symphony, or sitar, remember that while the words might be strange, the feelings are as familiar as a favorite song. Let's rock on!

7. How did one note cause the longest lawsuit in music?

The story of how one little note ignited the longest lawsuit in music history sounds like it could be the plot of a dramatic opera. It's all about a famous jazz pianist, Herbie Hancock, and another talented musician, Joe Zawinul. That single note comes from a track called "Cantaloupe Island," a jazz classic by Hancock from 1964. Jump ahead a few years, and Zawinul writes "In a Silent Way," bringing its own set of catchy tunes to the jazz scene.

The drama didn't play out on stage, though—it was a courtroom showdown. Hancock said that Zawinul's song borrowed one crucial note from "Cantaloupe Island," claiming it was essentially stealing. To most people, this might seem as minor as arguing over who first said "hello." But in music, a single note can make or break a song, kind of like a famous catchphrase everyone remembers.

When it comes to the law, music copyrights protect entire songs, not just single notes. So, you might wonder how one note could cause such a fuss. Turns out, it wasn't just any note; it was a key part of the song's identity—as unforgettable as a beloved movie quote.

Years of legal to-and-fro followed, like an endless game of musical chairs, but with no chairs actually removed. Finally, the courts had to decide what counted as inspiration and what counted as copying—a tricky dance that keeps lawyers busy.

What's fascinating here isn't just the legal stuff, but the strong feelings both musicians had for their work. It shows that in the world of art, even tiny details can mean a lot.

In a twist almost as satisfying as the perfect end to a symphony, the feud eventually wrapped up with a settlement. The lesson? Even in music, choose your battles wisely, or you might end up in a legal song with nothing but the rustle of court papers as the soundtrack.

8. How does a movie score play with your emotions?

When the lights dim and popcorn crunches, the music from a movie does more than play notes—it plays your emotions like a maestro with a baton. Notice how thrilling violins make your heart race, or how a sweeping orchestra in a love story tugs at your heartstrings? Movie scores guide your feelings more skillfully than a magician pulling rabbits out of hats.

Let's peek into the brain's backstage. The amygdala, a tiny almond-shaped part, is the emotional center that handles music. When it hears those creepy piano notes, it tells your body to gear up for fight or flight. Meanwhile, other brain areas scramble to figure out the story the music is telling. It's like having an internal team explaining why you should be biting your nails or grabbing tissues.

Different sounds trigger different feelings. Major chords, bright and happy, often play during triumphs or joy. Imagine a superhero zooming through the sky. Those glorious horns and strings scream they're about to save the day. In contrast, minor chords— deeper and sadder—signal tension or sadness. They set the stage for heartbreak or suspense, making sure you are glued to the screen.

Composers master the art of 'musical foreshadowing'. Think of "Jaws" with its ominous two-note theme. Just two notes, but they scream impending doom with the power of a full-blown monster in your living room. This primes you for what's next, keeping you on the edge of your seat.

And it's not just the notes. Volume and speed play big roles too. A sudden crescendo—a build-up of sound—can mimic a surprise. A slow, soft tune might wrap you in a comforting hug.

Next time you're watching a film, remember: the score is more than background noise. It's an emotional architect, shaping your moods without you realizing it. Just be glad they haven't scored a trip to the dentist yet!

In the end, movie scores are like secret directors, shaping your feelings with every note. When your heart races during an intense scene, tip your hat to the maestros behind the curtain—they know exactly what they're doing.

9. How did music piracy change the industry forever?

In the late 1990s and early 2000s, music piracy crashed into the industry like an unexpected drum solo at a quiet concert. Napster and its digital pals handed out free tunes faster than you could say "boombox," making CDs feel as old-school as a rotary phone. While artists and record labels worried about money slipping away, a quiet revolution began to hum in the background.

The internet morphed into a giant record store where everyone could browse, and, not surprisingly, this flipped the music business on its head. Before piracy, record labels controlled the market, holding onto it tighter than a guitar string. But with piracy, music became as easy to share as a funny cat video, whether you were in New York or New Delhi.

The industry, realizing the gig was up, had to get creative. It borrowed tricks from pirates and turned to streaming, matching the ease of piracy without the legal headaches. Enter Spotify and Apple Music, platforms that figured out how to make money from what people were already doing: endlessly enjoying songs. Now, people don't own music; they rent it, like an all-you-can-eat buffet.

The good news? A vibrant music scene where indie artists could find fans without selling out stadiums—or their souls. The bad news? The money musicians earn per stream is about as much as finding change under the couch cushions.

In short, piracy didn't kill music; it made it evolve. Like a rebellious teenager, it messed up, learned some lessons, and became something new and exciting. So, the next time you hit play on your favorite streaming app, remember the pirates from the past. They didn't just take music; they helped remix the whole industry.

10. How is silence a composer's secret weapon?

Silence in music might seem like an awkward pause in conversation, but for composers, it's more like the perfectly timed punchline in a joke. It turns out silence is much more than nothingness; it's a blank space full of possibilities—a composer's secret weapon.

Picture a melody as a roller coaster. The notes are the thrilling twists, but without those brief pauses—the silence—it would be a non-stop blur. Silence gives music its shape, helping listeners soak in what they've heard and wonder about what's next. It's the musical version of a deep breath, and sometimes, it's the silence between notes that truly makes the music sing.

Here's where science steps in. Our brains are great at filling in the gaps. When you hear a familiar tune, your brain often predicts the next note, creating a kind of mental music that dances in the quiet. This trick, called "closure," is why silence can be so powerful; it makes listeners an active part of the musical experience.

Silence is also perfect for building suspense. Think of a horror movie where silence hangs heavy—the lack of sound ramps up tension, making any sudden music all the more thrilling. In music, a quiet moment can heighten emotions, keeping listeners on the edge of their seats.

Silence even plays fair. It gives every instrument its turn in the spotlight, ensuring even the humble triangle or the quiet second violin gets to shine. By placing silences carefully, composers balance the music, making sure no one sound drowns out another.

At the end of the day, silence is more than just a pause. It's a canvas where composers craft their most detailed works, turning the absence of sound into a living part of their tunes. Next time you find yourself in a silent break during a song or symphony, don't let your mind wander. Lean in. Listen closely. The composer is saying a lot without a single sound. Sometimes, in music, less really is more!

11. How did music help bring down the Berlin Wall?

Music, it seems, could have given the Berlin Wall a real challenge in a showdown of rock tunes against concrete. The tale of how music helped take down the Wall is really about culture, catchy beats, and a non-stop will to rebel.

During the Cold War, East Germany wasn't exactly jamming to the latest hits. Western music was mostly banned, because nothing screams "strict regime" like outlawing The Beatles and Bruce Springsteen. But music has a clever way of sneaking through and dancing over walls—at least in spirit.

Western radio stations, like "Radio Free Europe," broadcasted rock and pop into the eager ears of East German youth. These young folks got creative, secretly tuning in and turning up the volume. Picture underground rock concerts right in their living rooms. The music sparked their dreams of freedom and made them think about what lay beyond the Berlin Wall.

Jump to 1987. Bruce Springsteen, the rock legend, performed in East Berlin. He played to 300,000 fans, all thrilled. This was a big deal, a political shake-up in a place where "Born in the USA" was not your usual sing-along. The concert became a call for change, and the excitement was unstoppable.

Music spoke a universal language, one that crossed the physical and ideological barriers of the Wall. It united people, spreading hope. In 1989, as the Wall finally fell, hammers and chisels weren't the only tools at work. The echoes of guitars and drums played their part too.

So, while music didn't literally knock down the Wall, it struck a chord that resonated with those craving change. Next time you're rocking out to your favorite song, remember: sometimes, the true power of music isn't just in the notes, but in its ability to break through walls—both real and imagined. Rock on!

12. How does music boost athletic performance?

Imagine this: You're jogging on a treadmill, each step feeling heavier than the last. Suddenly, your favorite playlist kicks in. Almost magically, your feet start moving to the beat. It feels like you could run forever. Is this some sort of wizardry? Not quite, but music's power to boost athletic performance can certainly feel magical.

When you listen to energizing tunes, especially those with a quick tempo, your brain releases dopamine. That's the same chemical that makes you happy when you eat chocolate or see a cute puppy. This boost can transform your workout from a chore to something fun. Music also distracts from the discomfort. When you're belting out your favorite song, you might forget your legs are begging for mercy.

This isn't just fun; it's science. Studies show that music increases endurance, power, and motivation. It's like having a personal cheerleader in your ear saying, "Keep going!" Your body naturally moves with the beat, a process known as "entrainment". Simply put, your body likes to match its rhythm to the music. It's like your body is saying, "I can dance to this!"

Choosing the right music matters. Fast, upbeat songs are great for high-energy workouts, while slower ones help with stretching. You wouldn't play a lullaby at a party if you want people to dance, right?

In the big show of working out, music is like a fairy godmother whispering, "You got this!" So next time you prepare for a tough workout, make sure your headphones are ready. With the right playlist, you might find yourself turning into a fitness star. Moving with new energy, stride by stride, note by note. Who knows? You might even start to enjoy it.

Myth Smashers

✖ MYTH:

You're too old to learn music.

✓ FACT:

It's never too late to learn music. Many adults find joy in picking up an instrument later in life. Just like starting a new hobby, it can be exciting and fun at any age.

✖ MYTH:

Music theory stifles creativity.

✓ FACT:

Music theory gives you the tools to be creative. It's like learning the alphabet before writing your story. It helps you explore more, not lock you in.

91 | WHY WHAT HUH?!

The WHENs

People haven't always been there for me but music always has.

— Jane Swan

1. When was the first music festival a hit?

The first music festival to really hit it big is a story best told with a guitar in one hand and a history book in the other. If we're thinking about music festivals like the ones today—big gatherings with tunes, mud, and way too many flower crowns—we have to go back to 1967. That was the Summer of Love, when the Monterey International Pop Festival rocked the scene in sunny California. Think of it like Woodstock before Woodstock, but with less mud and more sunshine.

The festival was a lineup of stars that could light up the night sky. Jimi Hendrix, Janis Joplin, and The Who all played there. Jimi Hendrix made quite the scene by setting his guitar on fire. This wasn't just a concert. It was a cultural explosion—a mix of music and the new counterculture movement that had everyone buzzing, in more ways than one.

So, why was Monterey such a big deal? Sure, the music was groovy, but it was more than that. The festival was a turning point where music became a tool for change. It sparked talks about peace, love, and freedom. It was like the crowd realized they were more than just fans—they were part of something big.

This event also changed how people saw music festivals. It showed they could be successful and still be all about creative expression. Fast forward a few decades, and festivals like Coachella and Glastonbury have taken up the torch—less guitar burning, but just as much excitement.

In a world where festivals are as common as coffee shops, it's cool to remember that it all started with a sunny weekend where music, change, and a little fire made history. The takeaway? Sometimes, "setting your guitar on fire" can spark something unforgettable.

2. When did the electric guitar electrify rock 'n' roll?

The electric guitar is as tied to rock 'n' roll as leather jackets and wild hairstyles. But when did this electrifying tool become the heartbeat of rock? The story kicks off in the 1930s, when musicians needed their guitars to be heard over the noisy big bands. Enter George Beauchamp and Adolph Rickenbacker, who started playing around with making guitars electric. Their first effort, called the "Frying Pan," was not quite rock-star material, but it was a beginning.

Fast forward to the 1950s. This is when the electric guitar truly entered the rock 'n' roll spotlight. Thanks to folks like Leo Fender and Gibson's Les Paul, who created guitars that looked cool and sounded even cooler. Think of the Fender Telecaster and Stratocaster, or the Gibson Les Paul. These were guitars that changed the game.

The electric guitar wasn't just about turning up the volume. It revolutionized music-making. Musicians like Chuck Berry, famous for his duckwalk and killer riffs, used it to wow audiences. Buddy Holly and Jimi Hendrix followed suit. They explored distortion, feedback, and sustain in exciting new ways. Like giving a painter a fresh set of colors and saying, "Paint the town!"

How does it work, you ask? Electric guitars use pickups—tiny magnets wrapped in wire—to turn string movements into electrical signals. These signals run through an amp to get that ear-bursting sound. Perfect for a stadium or ticking off your neighbor.

By the 1960s and 1970s, the electric guitar was the unchallenged ruler of rock 'n' roll. Bands like The Who, Led Zeppelin, and The Rolling Stones took it to legendary heights. Their riffs and solos became music icons. The electric guitar turned into a symbol of youth, rebellion, and pure creativity.

So, when did the electric guitar electrify rock 'n' roll? In the hands of the 1950s and 1960s trailblazers. And guess what? It's still rocking today. Proof that the simplest ideas can start a revolution. Now, where's my air guitar?

3. When did humans first dance to music?

Pinpointing when humans first danced to music is like searching for the start line at a really, really old dance marathon. We've been shaking our booties for ages—long before we had the smarts to jot down a date.

Our ancient ancestors didn't have Spotify, but they sure knew how to groove. Evidence suggests that early humans were dancing as soon as they realized they could move to a beat. Picture prehistoric folks, between their daily hunt and nap, breaking into a jig with nature's symphony—birdsong, thunder, or even the rhythm of handmade drums.

Cave paintings back them up. One in Bhimbetka, India, might be 9,000 years old, showing people dancing in a circle. Dance was already a part of life way back when.

But why dance? Apart from fun (which is reason enough), dance helped express emotions, tell stories, and even communicate with gods. It was social glue, bringing tribes together. Plus, it kept them fit—perfect for outrunning saber-toothed tigers.

Science hints that dancing is wired into our brains. It's linked to joy when movement and rhythm sync.

Dancing also helped early humans develop brain areas for language and abstract thinking. Who knew busting a move could be so smart?

In the end, while we can't date the first dance, we know it's as old as the hills—literally. So next time you hit the dance floor, remember: you're not just moving to the beat; you're part of something ancient. Dance like everyone in history is watching!

4. When did the saxophone jazz things up?

The saxophone first jazzed things up in the early 20th century. That's when it strutted its shiny brass curves onto the lively jazz scene. Even though Belgian instrument-maker Adolphe Sax invented it in the 1840s, the sax took its sweet time to find its groove. Imagine the sax as the slightly awkward newcomer at a party, waiting patiently for the perfect moment to shine.

Its big break came with jazz legends like Sidney Bechet and Coleman Hawkins. They saw the saxophone's potential to add some serious swagger and soul to their music. Jazz, born from the blues and ragtime, was just the right fit. The sax's versatility let it swoop and soar through playful improvisations; it was an instant hit. Think of it as the Swiss Army knife of instruments: equally at ease with a mellow tune or a wild jam.

By the Roaring Twenties, the sax was a jazz band staple. It added smooth and edgy flair to performances. If music had a cocktail party, the sax would be the guest grabbing all the attention, getting everyone dancing, whether in a smoky Harlem club or on a bustling New Orleans street.

Today, the saxophone is still a symbol of jazz. It continues to inspire with its ability to express deep emotions through every squeak and note. Next time you hear a sax solo that makes you tap your feet or snap your fingers, remember: this isn't just a sound. It's a century's worth of jazzing things up. Much like a saxophonist in the spotlight, it's endlessly fascinating and never out of style.

5. When did karaoke become a global craze?

Karaoke didn't hit the world like a surprise pop hit. It sneaked in, like an uncle who you're not sure can dance, but then steals the show.

In Japan, during the 1970s, karaoke—meaning "empty orchestra" in Japanese—started its journey. A musician named Daisuke Inoue, who was tired of playing the same old tunes, invented the first karaoke machine. His idea was simple: let the audience sing while he took a break. Sadly, he forgot to patent the device. That mistake was as unfortunate as singing off-key at a party, but it set the stage for karaoke's global fame.

The machine spread across Asia. In dimly lit bars and cozy living rooms, karaoke transformed shy singers into local stars. By the 1980s, it crossed into the United States. Americans fell in love with it quickly. Perhaps it was the lack of American Idol back then, which meant people could dream big and belt out tunes without judgment.

The big karaoke boom came in the 1990s and early 2000s. Karaoke boxes and bars popped up everywhere. They offered a space where anyone could sing their heart out. No judgment, just friends and maybe some forgiving walls.

Nowadays, karaoke is a global staple. It's on your phone with apps and in big international contests. It's even become a quirky tool for diplomacy—yes, "karaoke diplomacy" is a thing.

In short, karaoke's journey from Japan to the world is like a catchy song rising up the charts. It's an unexpected hit that shows everyone wants to be a rock star, at least for one night. It reminds us that while not everyone can sing like a legend, anyone can grab the mic and give it a shot. Remember, it's not about sounding perfect, it's about the fun of singing out loud.

6. When did MTV air its first music video?

MTV first hit the airwaves with a splash on August 1, 1981. Imagine a time when big hair and shoulder pads were all the rage. MTV decided to make its grand entrance with "Video Killed the Radio Star" by The Buggles. Talk about irony! This song was about how video would change everything, and they were absolutely right.

MTV started out in New Jersey, like a loud, colorful arcade filled with surprises. This first video was a peek into a new world where music was something you could watch as well as hear. The moment those synth notes played, a cultural shift began. People didn't just want to hear music anymore—they wanted the full visual experience.

MTV quickly became the center of cool. It changed fashion, talk, and even touched on politics. Music videos became more than just a way to sell songs—they were cultural landmarks. "Video Killed the Radio Star" predicted this change, with its catchy beat forecasting a move from just listening to watching music. MTV added a whole new layer to music, making watching it as exciting as listening.

If you're ever feeling nostalgic for when music videos ruled the world, remember it all started with a starry-eyed song and a video that mixed sounds with stories. In some alternate universe, if radio stars had never been "killed" by video, maybe we'd be tuning into MTV for our history lessons!

7. When did we first hear the spooky theremin?

The theremin: that strange instrument that seems straight out of a 1950s sci-fi movie or a classic haunted house. Its eerie sound has been tickling our ears for quite a while. But when did we first hear this ghostly music?

Imagine it's 1920. In Russia, a physicist named Léon Theremin (born Lev Termen) is busy experimenting in his lab. But he's not setting out to create a spooky soundtrack; he's actually trying to measure gas density. What he accidentally invents is truly unique: an instrument that plays without being touched. You just move your hands around its antennas, and it sings with a chilling voice that gives you goosebumps.

The first time people heard this odd device was in 1920 in Saint Petersburg, Russia. The audience? Likely a mix of amazement and mild terror, wondering if some kind of magic was at play. But it wasn't until the theremin crossed the Atlantic in the 1930s that it really began to make waves in music and pop culture.

In the late 1940s, the theremin's ghostly tones found a home in horror and sci-fi films. Remember movies like "The Day the Earth Stood Still" (1951) or

Hitchcock's "Spellbound" (1945)? The theremin was the real star, setting the mood with its chilling echoes.

So, while the first eerie notes of the theremin were heard over a century ago, its power to give us chills is still as strong as ever. It's the perfect no-touch instrument—ideal for anyone who loves spooky sounds without wanting to make contact. Whether crafting suspenseful movie scores or impressing friends with a mysterious no-touch melody, the theremin continues to intrigue us with its strange, otherworldly music.

8. When did streaming overtake album sales?

The moment streaming overtook album sales was a bit like when smartphones got smarter than calculators: it happened slowly, then all at once. Back in the mid-2000s, CDs were still the stars of the music world, spinning tunes in chunky boomboxes everywhere. But soon, people traded Walkmans for iPods, and suddenly, having a data plan became as common as owning a pair of headphones. Enter the digital revolution for music.

By 2016, streaming pulled ahead of album sales in the United States, marking a big shift in how we got our music. This wasn't just about new gadgets; it was a game-changer in our musical lives. Playlists took over record collections. Songs became just a tap away, no more trips to the record store needed.

Imagine this: music like a genie out of its lamp, roaming freely. Discover weekly playlists, endless radio stations, and more songs than you could ever count. The ease and access of streaming were music to everyone's ears. Music lovers? They adapted quickly, thrilled by the ocean of tunes available at a moment's notice.

Artists loved it too. Suddenly, they had a worldwide stage. No middlemen, just music. Debates about how to pay artists fairly? Still a hot topic, shaking the industry to its core.

In the end, streaming outpacing album sales was less of a fight and more like a remix. Technology changed our habits and how we enjoy music. So next time you hit shuffle on your playlist, remember: you're listening to the future. Keep those tunes turning and stay curious—it's the beat of what's next!

9. When did rap break into the mainstream?

Rap waltzed into the mainstream in the early 1980s, like a cool kid at a party who quickly becomes the center of attention. It sprouted at lively Bronx block parties in the late 1970s. But the big moment? "Rapper's Delight" by The Sugarhill Gang in 1979. This track wasn't just a tune; it was a cultural handshake, grabbing disco's beat and making everyone try their hand at rhyming—even if some were more clumsy than smooth.

The real game-changer came in 1986 with Run-D.M.C. and Aerosmith's "Walk This Way". Imagine mixing peanut butter with chocolate: two great tastes creating something even better. It was hip hop meeting rock, and it smashed into the charts. Music execs finally got it—rap wasn't a fleeting trend.

Then, by the late '80s and early '90s, stars like LL Cool J, Public Enemy, and N.W.A. pushed rap to new heights. The genre became more than just party music. It was a voice for storytelling and social change. Fast forward to 1990, and MC Hammer's "U Can't Touch This" had everyone dancing. It was a musical invite to a worldwide dance-off.

Before long, artists like Tupac and The Notorious B.I.G. weren't just on the charts—they owned them. Their songs were powerful stories that made people stop and listen.

So, when did rap break into the mainstream? It wasn't a single moment. It was a series of them. A catchy tune that got stuck in everyone's head. Today, rap isn't just in the mainstream—it's defining it.

Rap didn't just sneak into the mainstream. It built a home there, inviting everyone to join the party.

10. When was the first opera written and by whom?

Opera might seem like a world of dramatic plots and powerful voices, but its beginnings are quite a surprise. Picture this: Florence, Italy, late 16th century. A bunch of creative folks decided that music and theater should tie the knot. Opera was born—a bold mix with lots of vocal flair.

The first opera? That credit goes to Jacopo Peri, an Italian composer who probably didn't realize he was starting something huge. Around 1597, he penned "Dafne," which many call the first opera ever. It was performed for the crème de la crème of Florence, a group akin to a Renaissance book club. "Dafne" meshed music with drama in a way no one had seen before. Sadly, the music didn't survive, leaving us only with tales of its groundbreaking charm.

But Peri wasn't done. His next hit, "Euridice," came in 1600. This is the oldest opera we can still hear today. The story? Orpheus trying to save his love from the underworld. Perfect for opera lovers who adore a touch of myth and a lot of emotion.

Next time you're at an opera, or even just listening along at home, think back to those daring Italians.

Their leap of creativity paved the way for centuries of soaring arias and grand stages. Sometimes, all it takes to make history is a good tale, a little music, and a love for the dramatic.

11. When did vinyl records make a comeback?

Vinyl records are like the cats of the music world. They've got nine lives. Once thought to be outdated, vinyl made a surprising comeback around 2007. People had moved on to downloads and streaming. So, what brought vinyl back?

You can thank millennials, hipsters, and a big splash of nostalgia. As music went digital, folks began to miss the feel of holding an album and the unique sound only vinyl delivers. Listening to a vinyl record is an experience—like savoring a homemade meal versus munching on a protein bar.

Vinyl's warm tones and clear sound drew music lovers back. They rummaged through their parents' basements, brushing off old record players, and even bought new ones. Big-name artists and indie bands noticed. They began releasing their tunes on vinyl, turning these records into must-have items for fans.

Nostalgia is part of it, but there's a bit of science too. Vinyl records offer an analog sound that many believe better captures the original feel of a performance. Think of it like comparing a vivid painting to a digital copy. Both are good, but one has real soul.

Vinyl's return is also about connection. Endless streams of music can be overwhelming. Vinyl slows us down. It makes us appreciate music. We listen to whole albums, not just single tracks. It's like enjoying a full movie instead of watching clips on repeat.

In the end, vinyl's comeback is a blend of nostalgia, sound quality, and a yearning for something real in our music. So next time you're flipping through a record store, remember: vinyl never truly left. It just took a long, nostalgic pause.

12. When did live music become big business?

Live music becoming big business is a bit like a rock concert itself—full of a crescendo of historical milestones, bursts of business savvy, and, of course, a crowd-surfing pile of cash. Let's rewind to when live music was more about community fun than big bucks. In the early days, musicians were like the medieval Spotify. They were strolling minstrels and court performers who strummed lutes and livened up royal feasts, often getting paid with a pat on the back and maybe a chicken leg.

Fast forward to the roaring 1920s. Jazz musicians were drawing bigger crowds, playing in lively speakeasies and dance halls. But it was really the baby boomer era that put the "boom" in music. The 1960s saw bands like The Beatles and The Rolling Stones turning concerts into mega events. The "British Invasion" wasn't just on the radio; it brought hordes of fans eager to trade their pocket change for a live show. Promoters and ticket sellers quickly realized there was serious money to be made.

By the 1970s and 1980s, music festivals were sprouting everywhere—Woodstock, anyone?—transforming fields into temporary music havens. Then came MTV, making music truly global. Artists saw that performing live was no longer a side gig. It was the main event. Stadium tours became the norm, drawing in huge crowds, each ready to spend on tickets, T-shirts, and pricey snacks.

Today, live music is a giant in the entertainment world, with global revenues reaching billions. Technology has changed the game, with amazing light shows and fireworks that make performers seem like musical superheroes. Throw in the power of social media, and concerts are now not just about music. They're an experience. Perfect for Instagram.

So, when did live music become big business? It was a gradual build from medieval strummers to modern megastars, all tied together by our love for a good beat. In the end, music might be the world's oldest, most profitable magic. Who wouldn't pay to see their favorite tunes spring to life? Quite the encore, wouldn't you say?

Myth Smashers

✖ MYTH:

Overnight success is common in the music industry.

✔ FACT:

Most musicians spend years honing their craft. Like crafting a masterpiece or launching a business, success usually follows many unseen hours of hard work.

✖ MYTH:

Electronic music is easy to create.

✔ FACT:

Technology makes it accessible, but quality electronic music requires skill and imagination. Think of it like painting; the tools are there, but artistry is crucial.

The HUHs

Music is life itself.

- Taylor Swift

1. Huh?! Ever heard of a silent disco with headphone dancers?

Silent discos might sound like a puzzling idea, but they're very real and catching on at parties, festivals, and even museums. Imagine this: a room full of people dancing energetically, yet there's no music blasting from speakers. Instead, everyone's wearing wireless headphones, dancing to tunes playing directly in their ears while the space around them stays mysteriously quiet. It's a dance party you can only hear if you join in.

The secret to a silent disco? Those wireless headphones. Each person can usually switch between different channels, picking which DJ or playlist they want to jam to. It's like having your own private club where you call the shots on the music. This not only keeps noise complaints away but lets all sorts of musical tastes exist side by side. Picture someone bouncing to the latest pop hit right next to another person enjoying classical tunes—silent discos make it happen!

Here's the fun part. Silent discos play with our love for both tech and togetherness. It's as if you're dancing to your own beat, yet part of a bigger group. It's a cool way to show how we use technology to connect and keep the peace.

And don't forget the fun of watching a room full of people dancing in silence. It's a show all on its own— a quirky dance of the headphone crowd. For the curious among us, a silent disco invites you into a strange, yet together, world. The tunes are private, but the fun is shared. So, if you find one, don't just hear about it—dive in and join the fun. It's the most exciting silence you can experience!

2. Huh?! Why do some frogs drum like percussionists?

Imagine wandering through a rainforest. Suddenly, you hear a series of thumps. It sounds like a jungle band is playing. But hold on! The musicians are little frogs. Yes, frogs have their own drumming gigs.

These drumming frogs, especially the "foot-flagging frogs," aren't just jamming for laughs. They're talking. In the noisy rainforest, where all kinds of animals are chattering, getting heard is tricky. Some clever frogs have come up with a special trick. They use their feet to drum on leaves or their own bodies. This sends vibrations through the air like a natural telegram.

So, why make all this noise? The main reason is love—or at least finding a mate. Male frogs put on these rhythmic shows to catch the eye (or ear) of a mate. The more stunning the beat, the more likely they are to impress. It's like nature's version of speed dating. First impressions? All in the beat.

Drumming has another job too: marking territory. Frogs, like some people, can be quite territorial. By drumming, they tell other males to back off. Otherwise, they might have a rhythm battle on their hands.

This drumming goes back to how they've evolved. Frogs are great at picking up vibrations. This helps them find partners and dodge danger. It's a survival trick that also works for flirting. Nature sure knows how to multitask.

So, when frogs drum, they create a mix of survival and romance. It's a fascinating mix of biology and sound. Next time you hear a beat in the jungle, think of these tiny drummers. They show us that sometimes winning hearts—or just a quiet spot—takes a strong rhythm and an undeniable beat.

3. Huh?! Can plants really groove to tunes and grow better?

Imagine a world where plants are the ultimate party guests, swaying to the beat while sprouting new leaves. Picture a leafy disco scene. But can plants really boogie to music and grow better? Let's explore this green mystery, one beat at a time.

In the 1970s, a book called "The Secret Life of Plants" suggested that playing a bit of Bach or Beethoven could make your ficus as happy as a clam. People started playing music to their plants, hoping for a symphony of sprouts. Curious, right?

Science enjoys poking around such ideas with a big magnifying glass. Some research hints that plants exposed to certain sounds might grow more. For example, one study in South Korea found that playing classical music to rice plants increased their yield. But before your spinach gets a playlist, remember: it might be the vibrations rather than the music itself that matter.

Plants don't have ears or brains like us, but they can pick up on vibrations. Sound waves create tiny shakes in leaves that might trigger growth. Plants might feel the music rather than hear it.

Not all music is equal in the plant kingdom. Classical tunes could be a winner, but heavy metal might just be noise to your petunias. Plants might prefer soothing sounds—think of it as a spa day for them.

In nature's grand concert, plants march to their own drum. They might not dance like us, but they respond to the world around them in their own unique way. So, while your cactus may not headbang to rock, a gentle lullaby might give it extra pep.

Next time you hum a tune while watering your ferns, you might just be adding a sprinkle of joy. Whether it's the music or just your loving care, your plants could be smiling in their own quiet way. Keep the tunes rolling and let your garden decide if it's a fan. After all, everyone's a critic—even your begonias!

4. Huh?! There's a record for a concert lasting 453 hours?

You heard right—there really is a record for a concert that lasted 453 hours! That's almost 19 days of non-stop music. Imagine a show so long that even a night owl would need a nap. This record was set by a group of musicians eager to test their endurance. Think about performing longer than it takes to binge-watch Friends several times. Without a nap break.

How do you keep a crowd interested for such a marathon of music? A dash of creativity, heaps of variety, and plenty of energy help. These musicians likely found clever ways to keep folks awake. Maybe they mixed up the music styles or turned the stage into a mini-festival. The playlist must have been long—longer than a list of scary movies for a sleepover.

Pulling off a concert like this requires careful planning. Lots of backup musicians and a saintly patience from anyone listening to the same drum solo again and again. Guinness World Records keeps a close eye to make sure no one dozes off mid-song. But some caffeine and snacks probably came in handy too.

In the end, a 453-hour concert isn't just about records. It's about passion and human endurance. And maybe about pushing music to its limits. So next time you're at a live show that feels like it's dragging on, remember—it could always be longer!

5. Huh?! Why did a symphony have people break stuff?

When you think of a symphony, you might picture grand concert halls, fancy outfits, and the soft clink of glasses. So, why were people breaking stuff at one? Let's jump into this musical mystery.

Imagine an orchestra where violins team up with... metal pipes and hammers. Sounds odd, right? It's not a comedy sketch, but a peek into the world of avant-garde music. In the early 1900s, composers like Edgard Varèse and John Cage wanted to shake things up. They stretched beyond regular instruments, challenging our ears and making us rethink music.

Enter "destructive music," where everyday noises—even breaking objects—become part of the show. A famous piece by John Cage, "4'33"," had performers not playing a single note, leaving listeners to notice every cough and shuffle. Others went for a more literal bang, blending sounds of smashing and crashing into their works. It was raw and definitely new.

Why would they do this? These composers aimed to get us thinking about what music is. Is it just sweet sounds, or can it express raw, unfiltered feelings? By using the noise of breaking things, they pulled the audience into the act, mixing art with real life.

Picture it like a musical treasure box, pushing us to explore what we call music. The chaos? It makes us listen in fresh ways and find surprising beauty in everyday noise.

Next time you hear about breaking things at a symphony, nod with understanding. Breaking the rules sometimes creates new tunes. Who knew a smashed plate could be music to our ears? It's a smash hit of a symphony!

6. Huh?! Can music change how food tastes?

Imagine biting into a juicy burger while a symphony of Beethoven plays around you, turning each bite into an orchestral adventure. It's not just a culinary fairytale—music can actually change how food tastes.

This mix of sound and taste falls under multisensory experiences, a fancy way of saying our senses like to work together. Scientists, particularly Charles Spence from Oxford University, have been exploring how music can tweak our taste buds. High-pitched sounds make things taste sweeter, while deep bass notes bring out bitterness. Think of it as an audio seasoning that changes the flavor just by adjusting treble or bass.

Some restaurants are getting in on the act, pairing meals with playlists. Imagine eating sushi with soft strings and ocean sounds—the fish seems fresher, the wasabi milder. Could this be why cheap wine suddenly feels fancy with a few operatic tunes?

This isn't just your brain playing tricks. Our minds are like that chatty friend who overhears everything. When they catch a tune, they can change how we taste food. It's like your taste buds are at a concert and a spoonful of soup becomes the star performance.

So, next time you sit down for dinner, think about your soundtrack. With the right notes, your meal might just hit a high note. Bon appétit and happy listening!

7. Huh?! Why does a song play nonstop in a Hawaiian lava tube?

Imagine you're exploring a Hawaiian lava tube, one of those mysterious tunnels shaped by flowing lava. Suddenly, you hear a familiar tune repeating endlessly, echoing through the cave. Did you accidentally stumble into a quirky art project?

Here's what's happening: Hawaiian lava tubes, those underground tunnels formed from flowing lava, have unique acoustics. They trap sound waves, bouncing them around like a fun game of ping pong. It's not magic, but it sure feels like it when a sound gets caught and repeats, making it seem like a song is playing nonstop.

If a melody—or any noise—slips inside a lava tube, it can stick around like gum on a shoe. The combination of smooth, hard walls and the tube's shape can amplify the sound, much like a concert hall carries music beautifully. So, if someone hums a little tune, the lava tube might just become its own DJ, looping the sound over and over.

But why does this happen specifically in lava tubes? The special structure of these tubes plays a big role. The hard basalt rock doesn't soak up sound well, so instead of fading away, the sound waves keep bouncing back and forth until they eventually vanish. Think of it as nature's own echo chamber, but with more lava involved in the making.

Interestingly, this acoustic trick is much more likely in empty lava tubes. When they're filled with rocks or water, the sound waves can't bounce around as effectively. Next time you stroll through one of these natural corridors, try singing a little song and enjoy the volcanic playlist.

In the end, while a Hawaiian lava tube might not be the next big music venue, it offers a surprising symphony that turns nature's quirks into a show worth hearing. Who knew lava could get into the groove so well?

8. Huh?! Did you know there are beetles named after famous musicians?

Imagine wandering through the wondrous world of bugs and coming across a beetle with a rock star's name. Sounds like fiction? In the world of science, truth is indeed stranger—and more fun—than fiction. Meet the beetles named after famous musicians. They are as small as a guitar pick, yet their names echo as loudly as your favorite tunes.

Scientists, with a knack for creativity, sometimes name new species after cultural icons. It's their fun way of nodding to the music legends who've made waves in the world. Consider the Agra schwarzeneggeri, though not a musician, this beetle gives a playful salute to the action hero. More on the musical side is the Scaptia beyonceae, a fly with a "bootylicious" golden back, much like Beyoncé's iconic style.

There was also the Anophthalmus hitleri, named after a historical figure that turned out to be a not-so-great choice. This highlights the need for thoughtful naming. Today, scientists aim for names that bring a smile rather than a frown. A beetle named Beetle McCartney? Or Lady Buggaga? Why not!

Naming beetles after famous people isn't just for laughs. It helps draw attention to the importance of bugs and their role in nature. Plus, it gives us a delightful mix of science and pop culture, making even the tiniest creature shine in the spotlight.

Next time you hum your favorite song, think of the beetles. They're not playing in any bands, but they are little stars in their own way. Who knows? The next beetle discovery might just bear the name of your favorite artist. Until then, let your curiosity buzz and your eyes stay wide open—there's a world of wonders waiting for you to unearth.

9. Huh?! Can a song be dangerous at certain frequencies?

Imagine you're at a concert. The bass is thumping, your heart is beating fast, and you think, "This music is really intense!" Well, in some ways, certain frequencies might be just that! It sounds like something from a sci-fi movie, but the idea that a song could be "dangerous" at certain pitches isn't all fiction.

Let's dive into the science pool. Our ears handle a lot—from the lovely morning bird songs to the not-so-lovely vacuum cleaner noise. But there's a range of pitches—those super low, rumbly ones—that can do strange things to our bodies. Infrasound, which means sound waves under 20 Hz, usually hides below our hearing range. But just because we don't hear it doesn't mean it doesn't affect us.

Infrasound can make us feel rather than hear. Have you ever felt creepy in an old house? That might be infrasound, making you feel uneasy or even a bit sick. The famous "brown note" myth claims that some low sounds might cause, let's say, tummy troubles. While there's no solid proof for this tale, it remains a fun urban myth.

Then there's "resonance." Everything has a natural frequency, even humans. If a sound matches this frequency, it might make things—like a bridge, glass, or your ears—vibrate wildly and maybe even break. But before you picture buildings falling to a DJ's drop, know that such events are rare and not as dramatic as in the movies.

In certain areas, like military tactics or crowd control, infrasound has been tested as a way to confuse or move people. But these uses are secretive and definitely not the kind of playlists you'd find on Spotify.

So, relax and enjoy your favorite tunes without worrying about sudden explosions. It's fascinating to think about sound's hidden power. Next time you feel the beat, remember: those low sounds aren't just giving you rhythm—they're making you feel something deeper. Isn't that what music is all about?

10. Huh?! Why do little birds mimic musical instruments?

Little birds mimicking musical instruments might seem like they're prepping for a gig as the next big bird band, but there's more to it than meets the ear. These feathered performers, like Australia's superb lyrebird, aren't just showing off their vocal skills for fun. It's a smart survival trick.

In the wild, standing out with a unique song is both a blessing and a curse. It can attract a mate impressed by the originality, but it can also draw in predators. So, what's a little bird to do? They copy sounds around them—chainsaws, camera clicks, and yes, even musical instruments.

This mimicry is like rolling out the red carpet for potential partners. A male bird that imitates many sounds is telling a female, "Look at me! I'm talented and adaptable!" It's nature's version of serenading someone with a perfect mixtape.

But that's not all. Mimicking sounds can trick predators, turning the bird into a master illusionist. It might make it seem like there are more birds or even bigger creatures nearby, keeping threats at bay.

These birds aren't just nature's echo boxes; they're clever strategists using this trick to survive and thrive. So next time you hear a bird that sounds like your favorite music, remember—it's not hunting for a record deal, it's playing the smart survival game. Who knew birds could rock the forest like that?

11. Huh?! A city once got fined for being too quiet?

Imagine a city fined for being too quiet—it sounds more like a joke than reality, right? But let's tiptoe into the quirky story of Monza, a charming town in Italy, that faced just this bizarre situation.

In 1897, Monza, sitting pretty in the Lombardy region, decided it wanted to be even quieter. Known for its peaceful parks, the town passed a law to ban any noise that might disturb the calm. Sounds sensible, until you realize the twist: the rule was so strict that it even silenced the city's cleaners. No broom clattering allowed! The streets couldn't be swept without making some noise. The result? Dirt piled up faster than the city could silently brush it away. And yes, Monza got fined because of it!

This curious case shows how aiming for total silence can turn into a messy affair, like trying to eat spaghetti with a spoon. In our noisy world today, many cities are still looking for smart ways to cut down on noise without losing their vibrant hum.

So next time you're told to keep quiet, think of Monza. Here's a town that took "silent, please" a touch too far—and paid the price. Just a fun little reminder that even silence, our peaceful friend, can sometimes make a bit too much noise!

12. Huh?! Can music be used as money, and has it ever?

Imagine walking into a store and, instead of pulling out cash or your trusty credit card, you start humming your favorite tune. Sounds like a scene from a quirky musical, right? The idea of music as money isn't completely out there. While you won't be paying for your groceries with a catchy chorus today, music has played a role in economies and trade in some pretty interesting ways.

Think about medieval Europe. Back then, wandering musicians like troubadours and minstrels traveled from village to village. They'd perform songs and tell tales in exchange for food, shelter, or sometimes even a few coins. Their melodies acted as a kind of currency—a lyrical barter system. Sing a song, get a meal. Pretty neat!

Jump ahead to the era of vinyl records. Music turned into actual gold. Selling millions of records translated to "gold" and "platinum"—markers of success and wealth. It wasn't cash in your hand, but music was clearly exchanging for money, loud and clear.

Now, think about digital platforms like Spotify. Here, music has become a service generating income.

Countless plays and streams turn into money. You can't use your playlist to pay rent, but when you listen to that catchy pop song on repeat, it's generating tiny fractions of money for the artist. Kind of like a modern-day minting process.

What about music as real currency? With the rise of cryptocurrencies and NFTs (non-fungible tokens), we get closer. Artists sell unique digital albums or tracks, much like collector's items or shares. It's a new frontier.

To sum it up, while you might not trade a Beethoven symphony for a loaf of bread just yet, music has woven itself into our economy in clever ways through the ages. So, next time you tap your feet to a tune, just remember: you're part of a melody with money magic. And who knows? Maybe one day you'll pay for your cappuccino with a chorus. Until then, keep on humming!

Myth Smashers

✗ MYTH:

Music classes are only for children.

✓ FACT:

Adults can gain just as much from music classes. Learning music at any age boosts brain skills. Plus, it's a fun way to spend time, just like yoga or pottery.

✗ MYTH:

Music therapy is just musical entertainment.

✓ FACT:

Music therapy is a serious healing practice. It aims to boost emotional health and mental skills, not just entertain. It's like physical therapy for your mind and soul.

WHY WHAT HUH?!

Printed in Great Britain
by Amazon